World of Dogs Adult Coloring Book

This book belongs to:

____

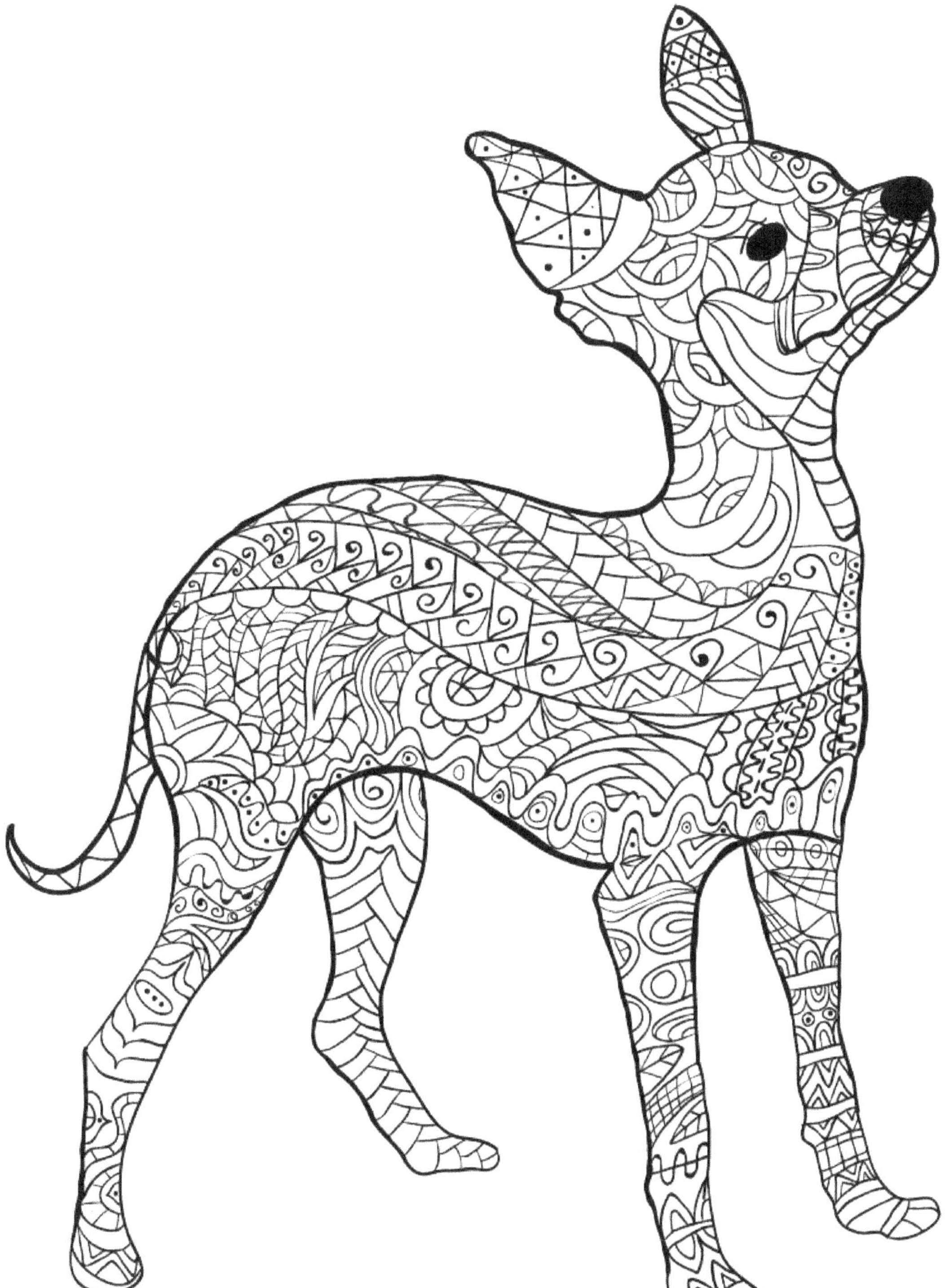

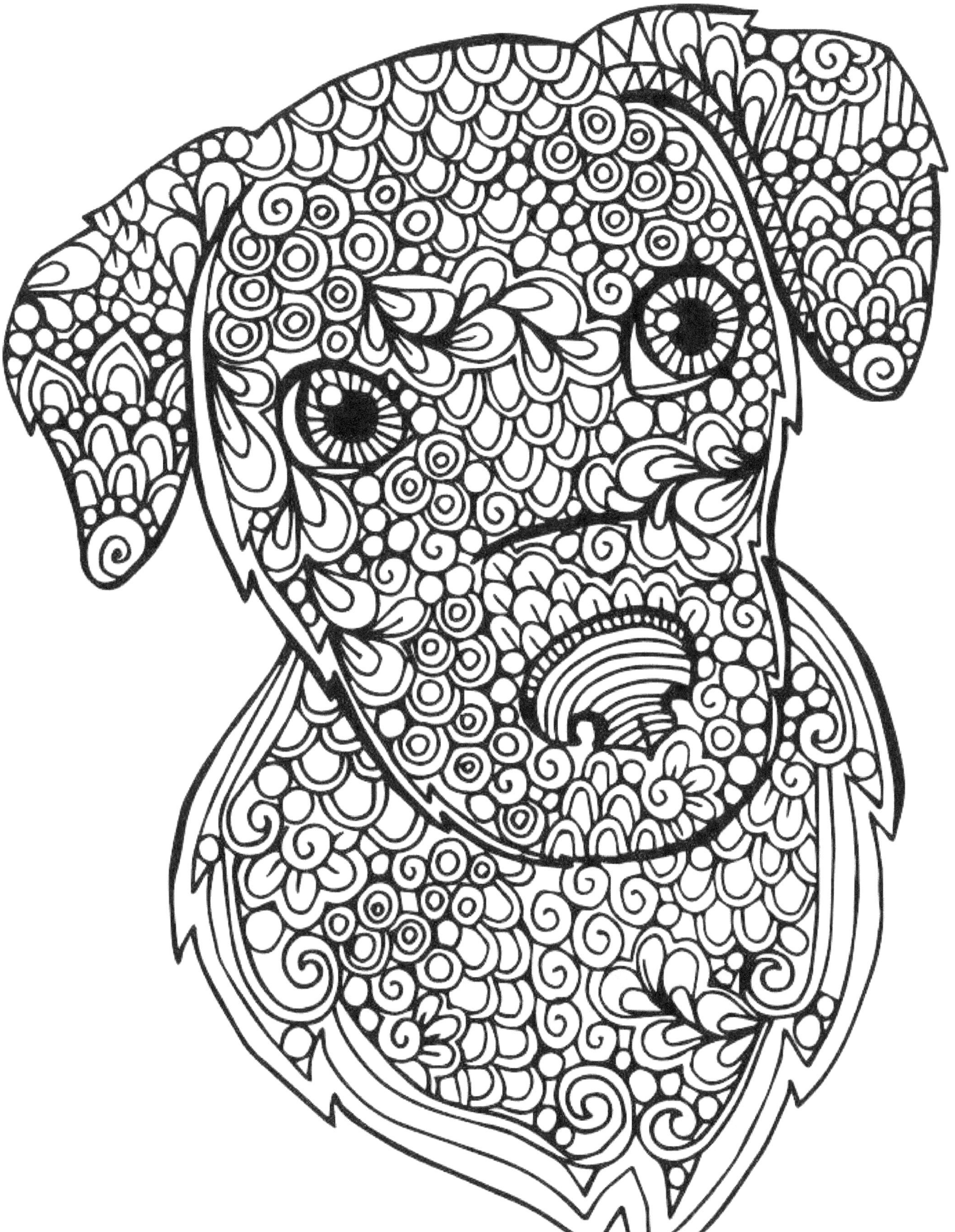

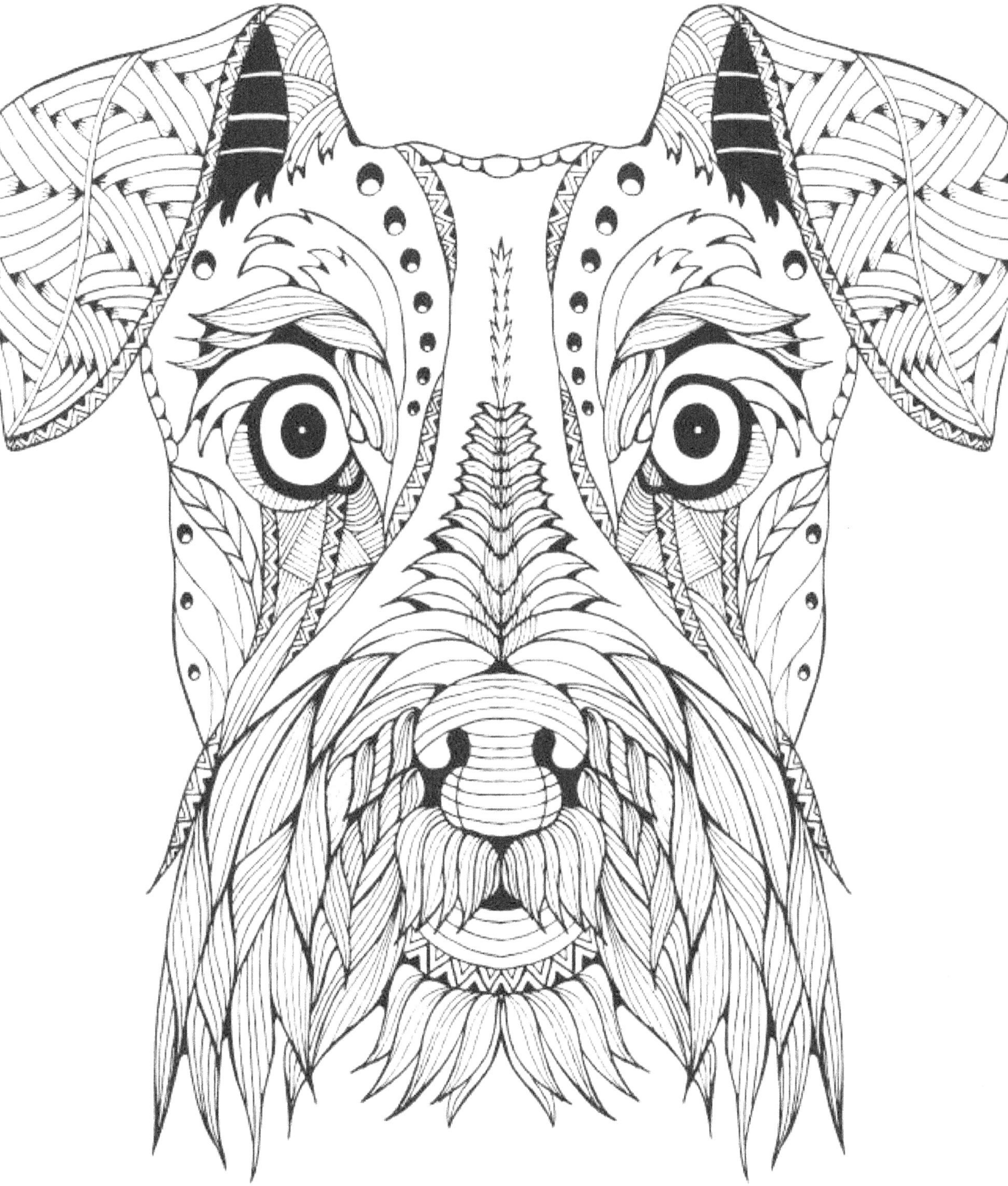

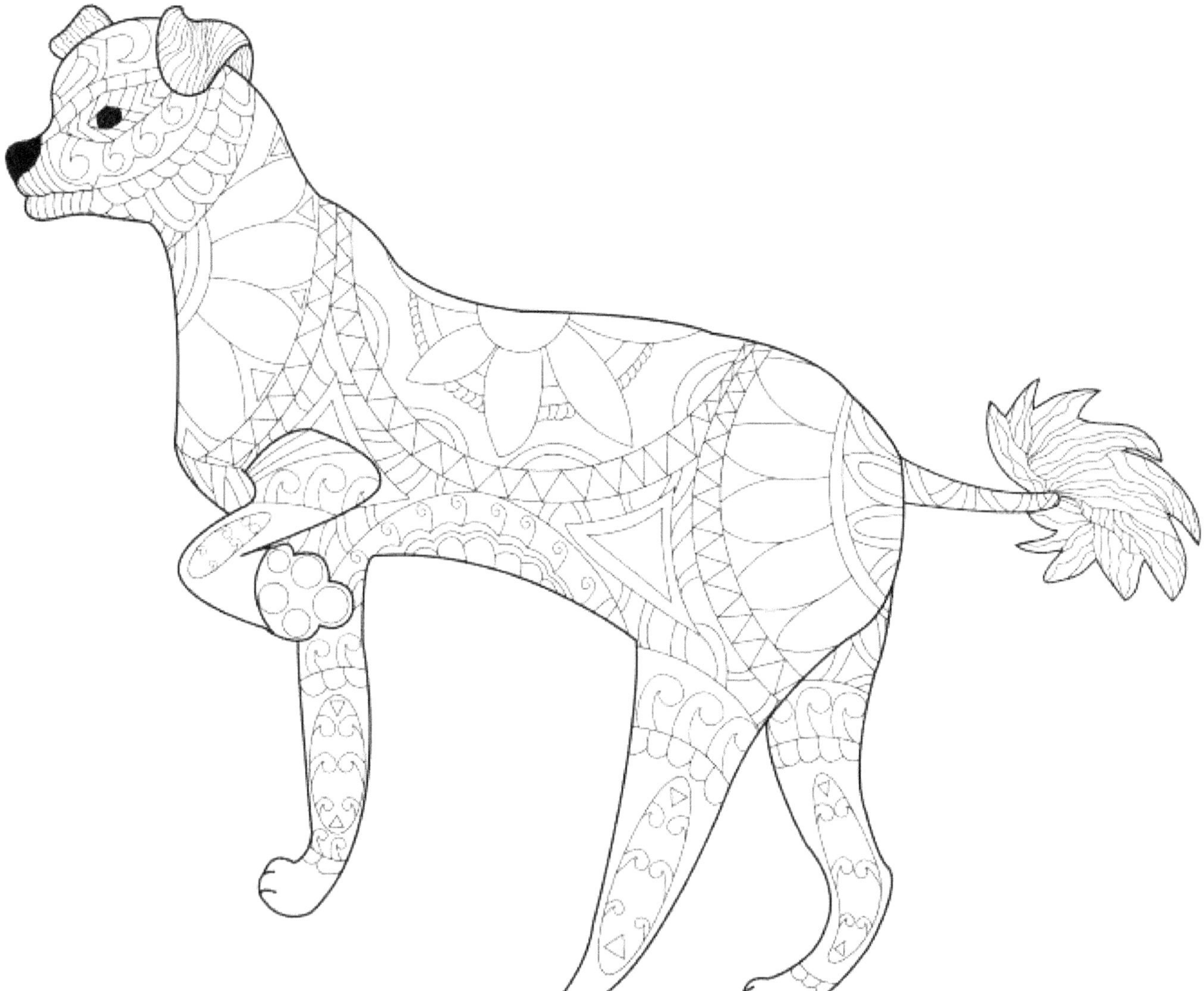

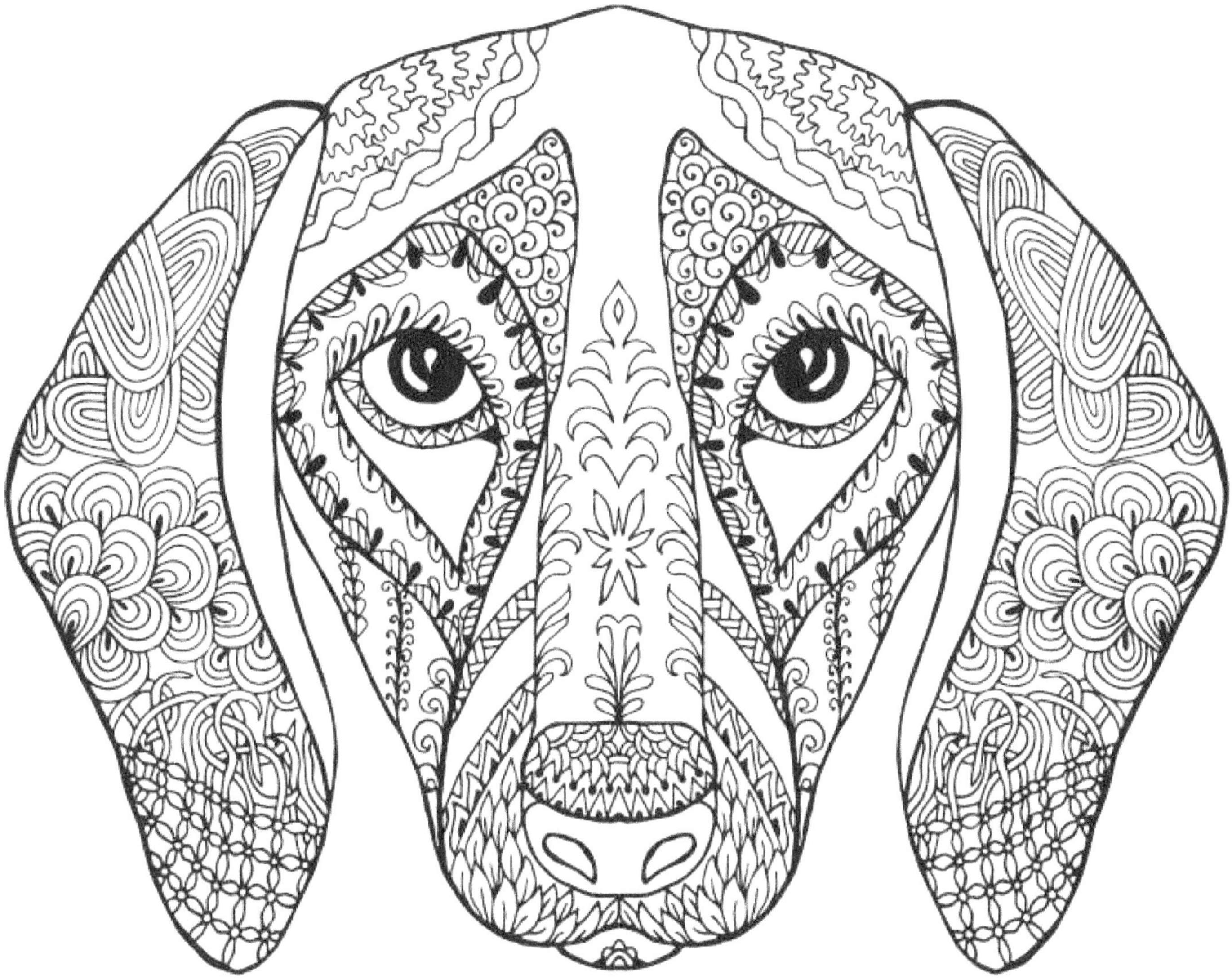

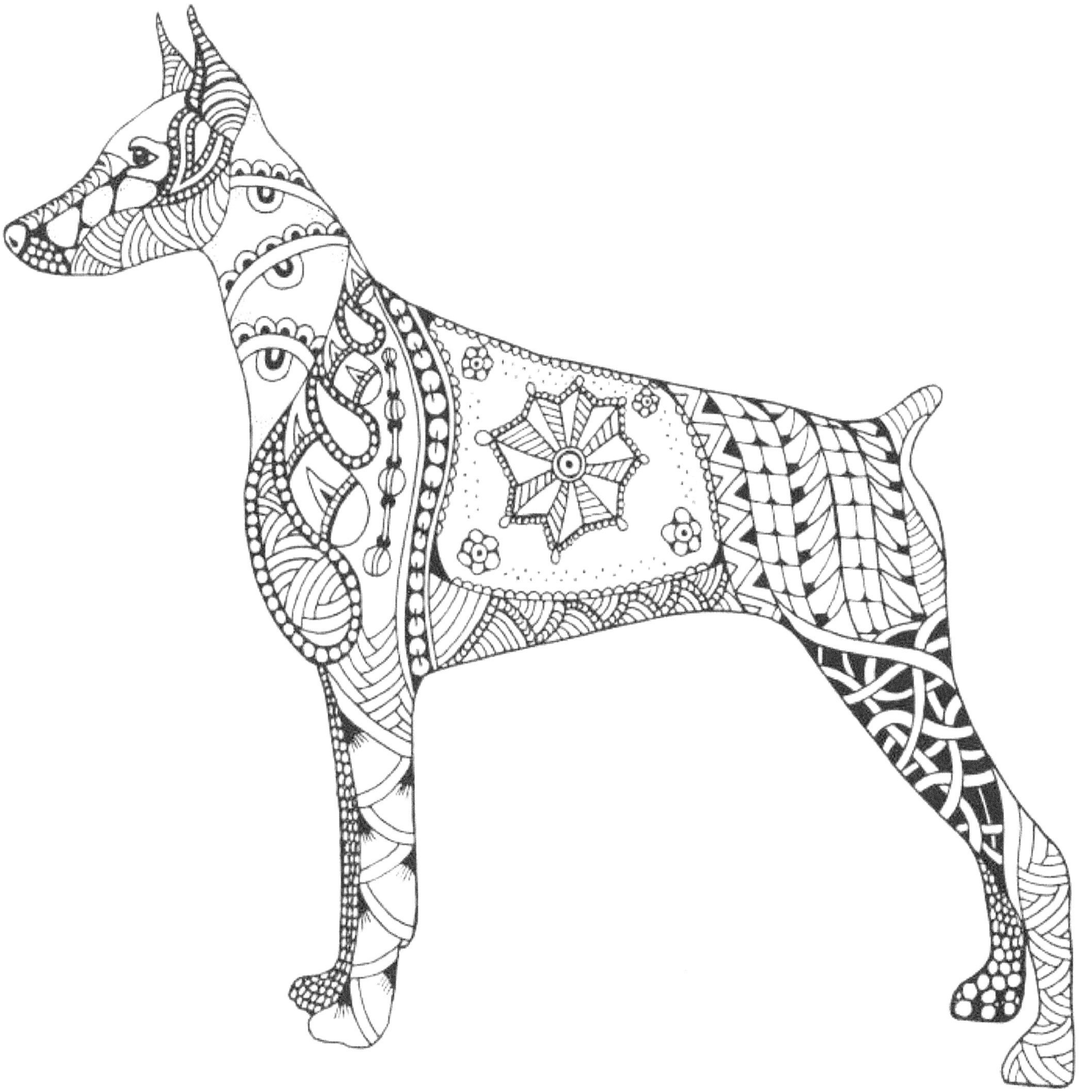

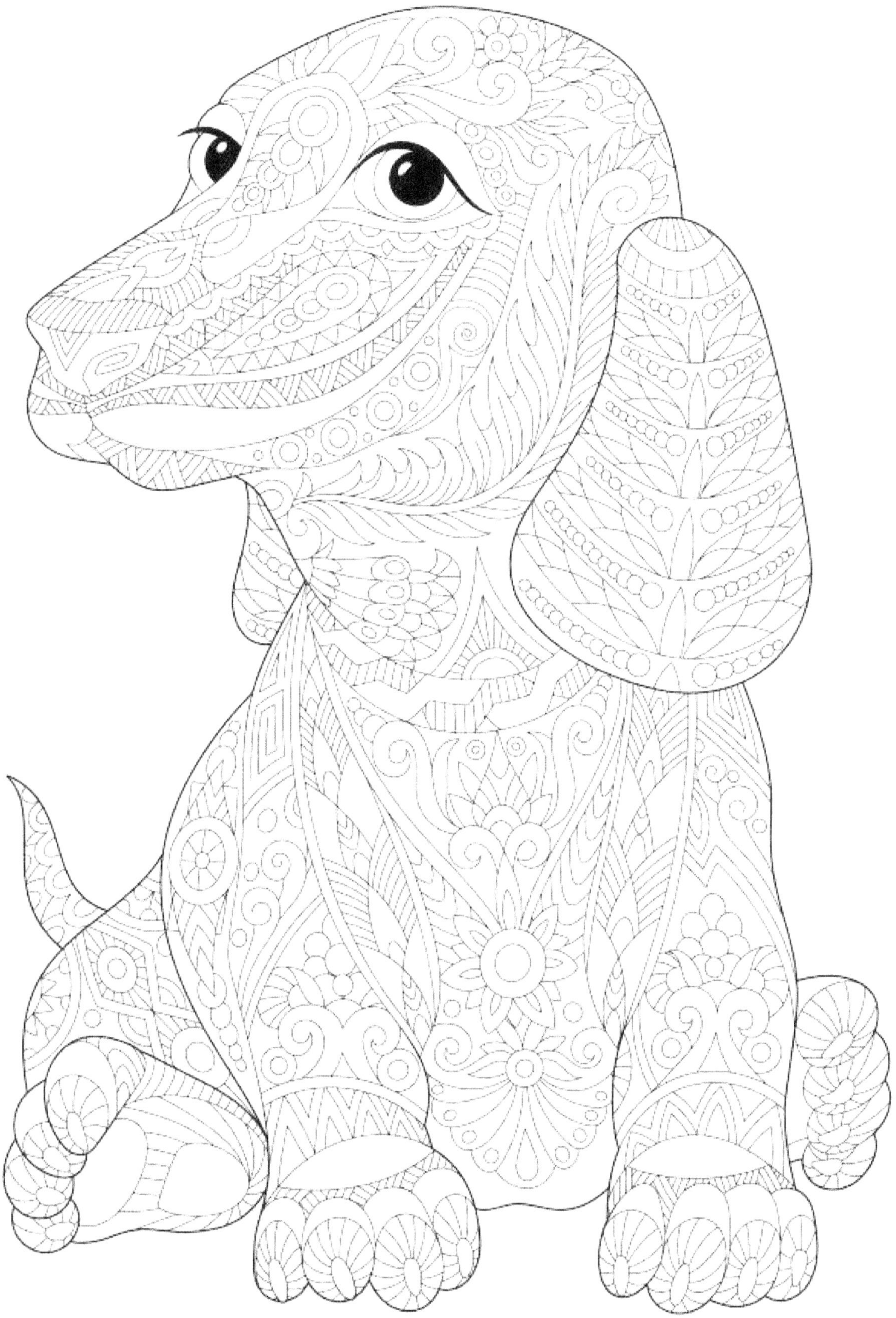

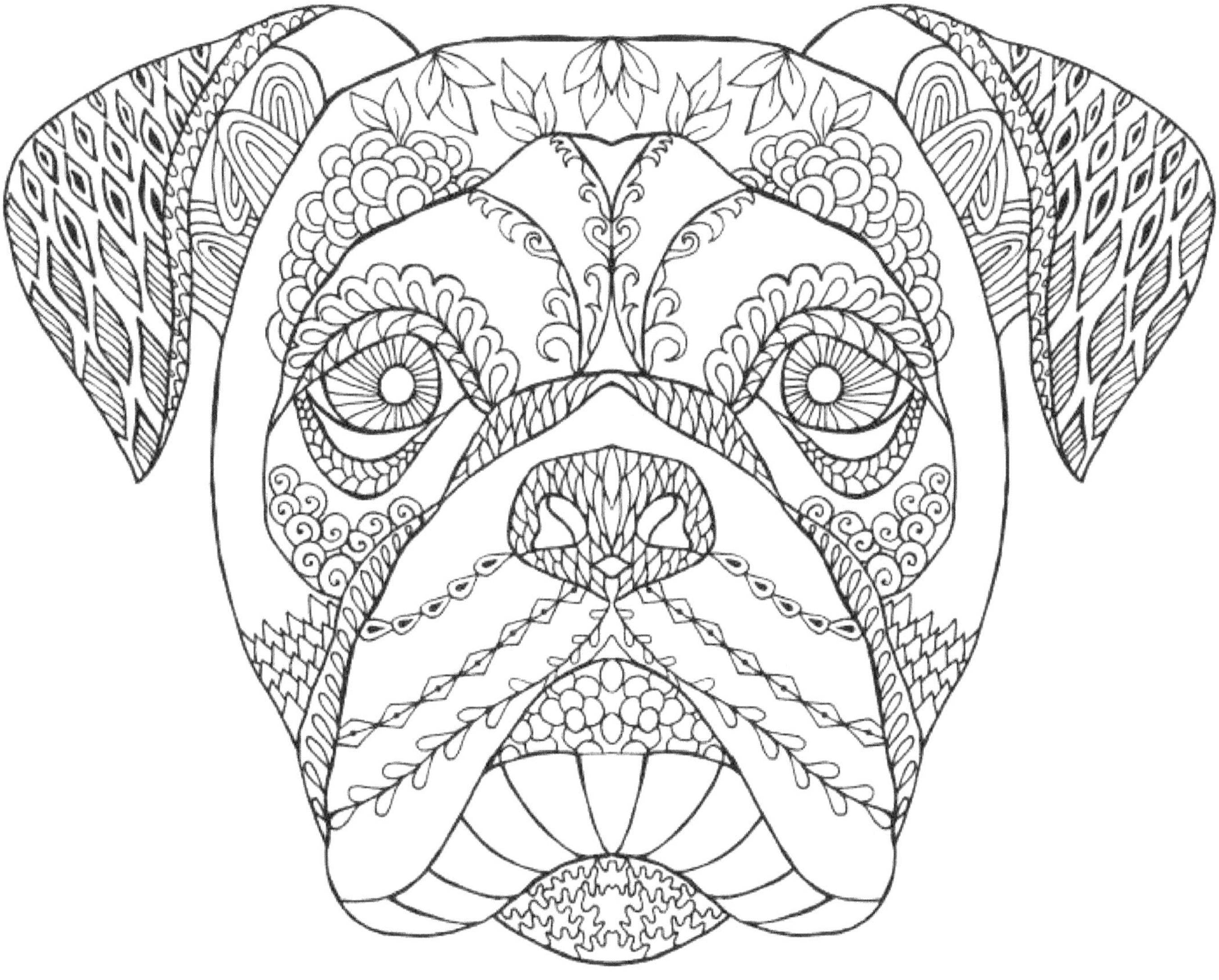

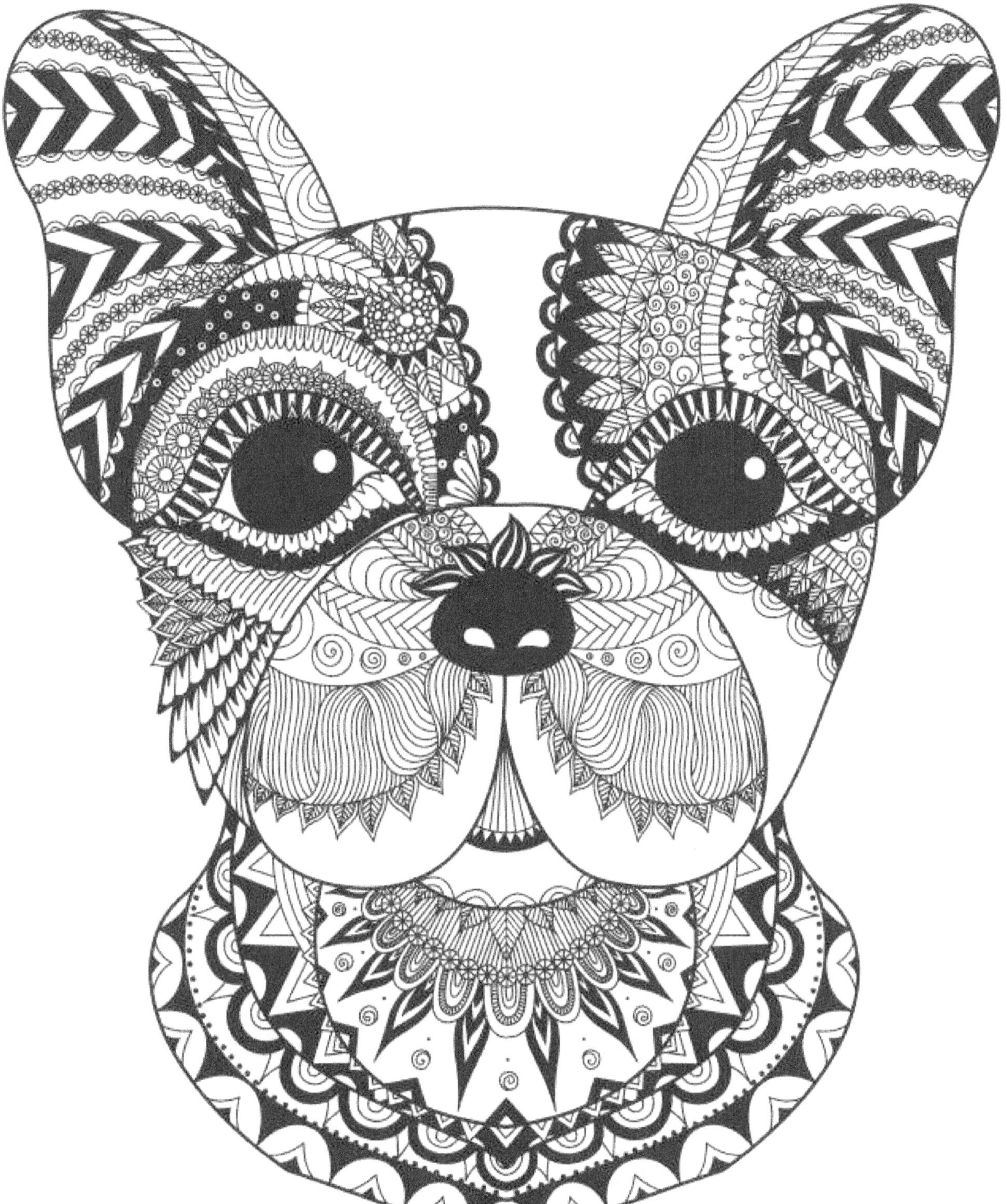

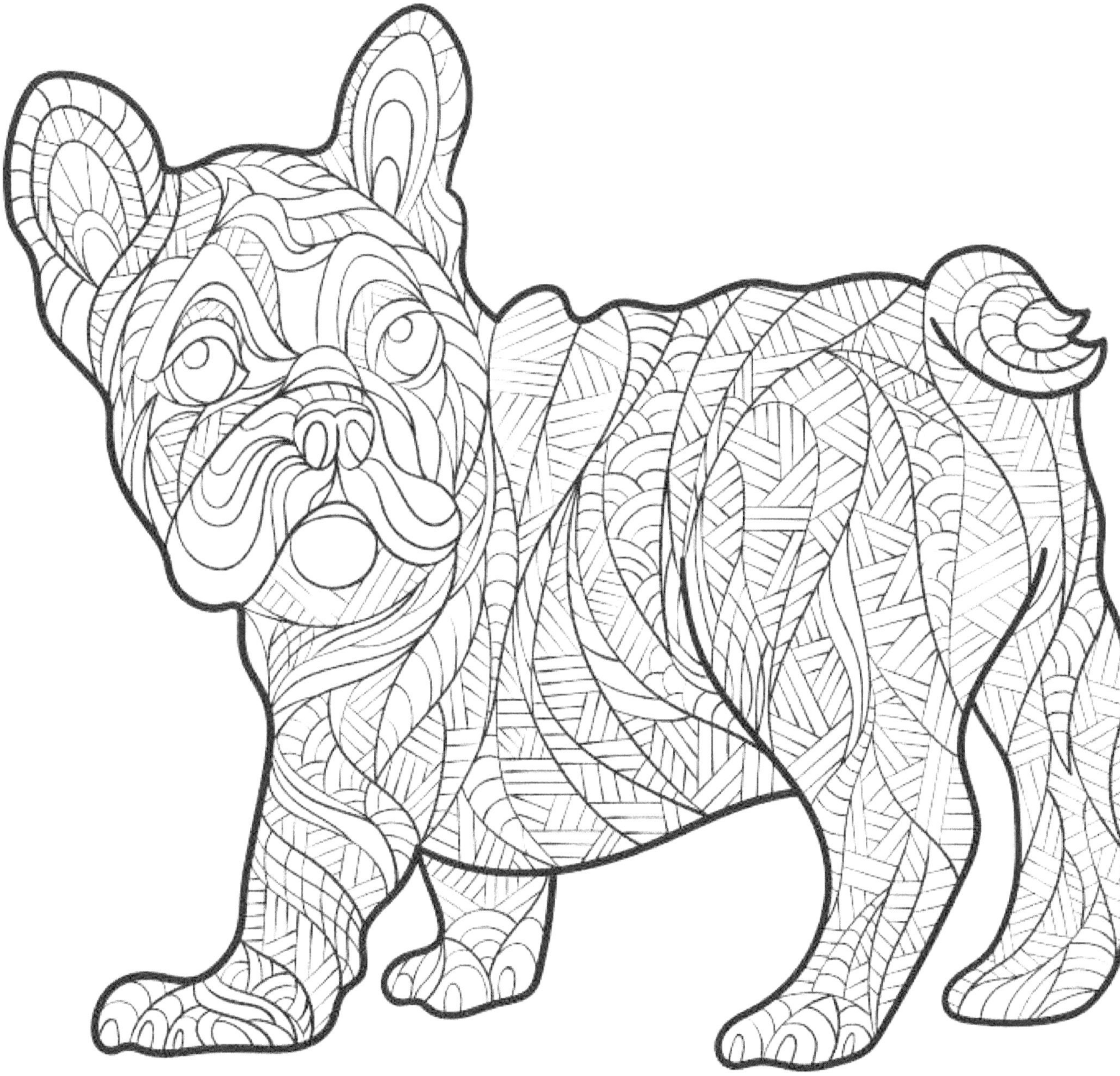

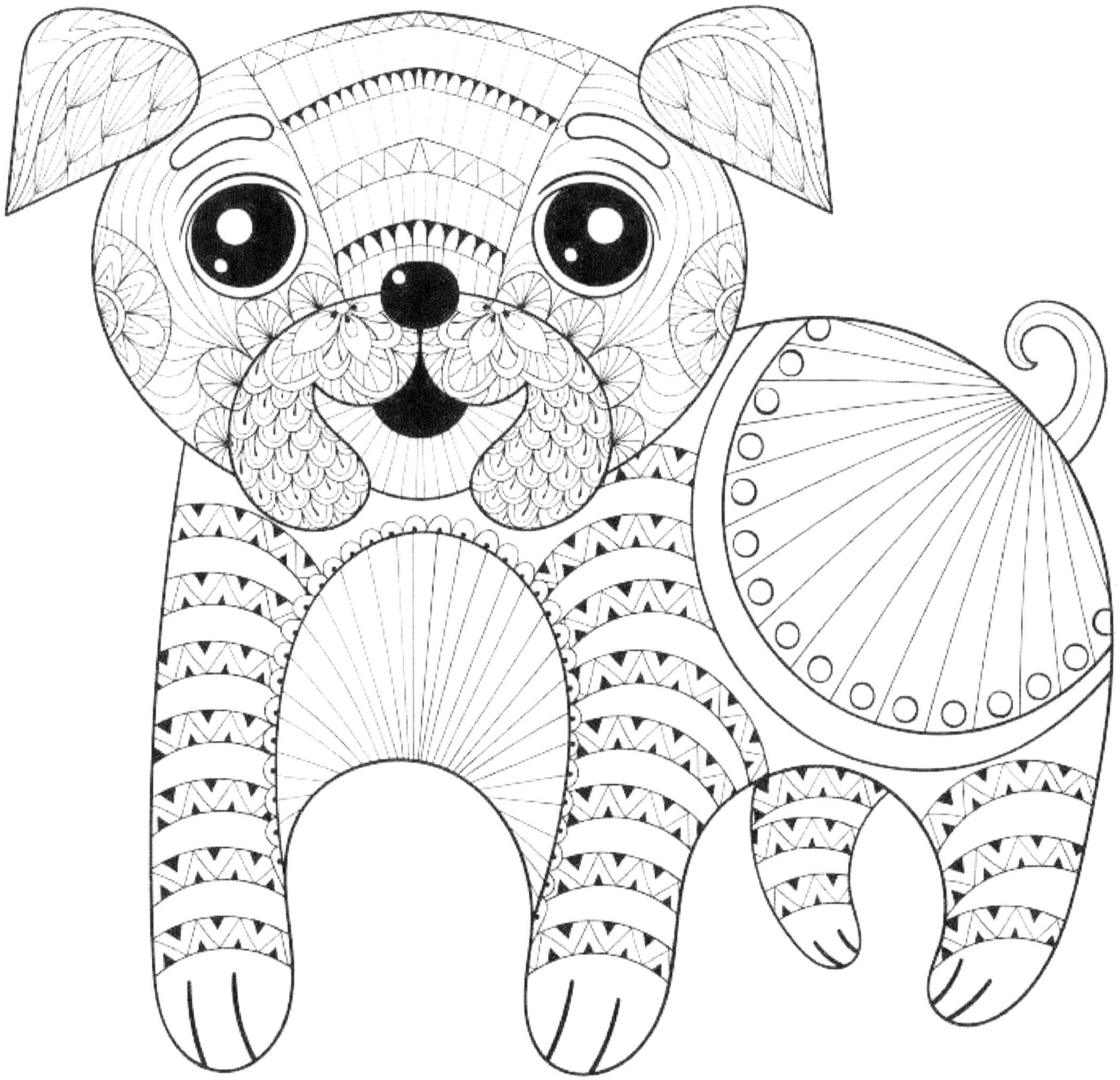

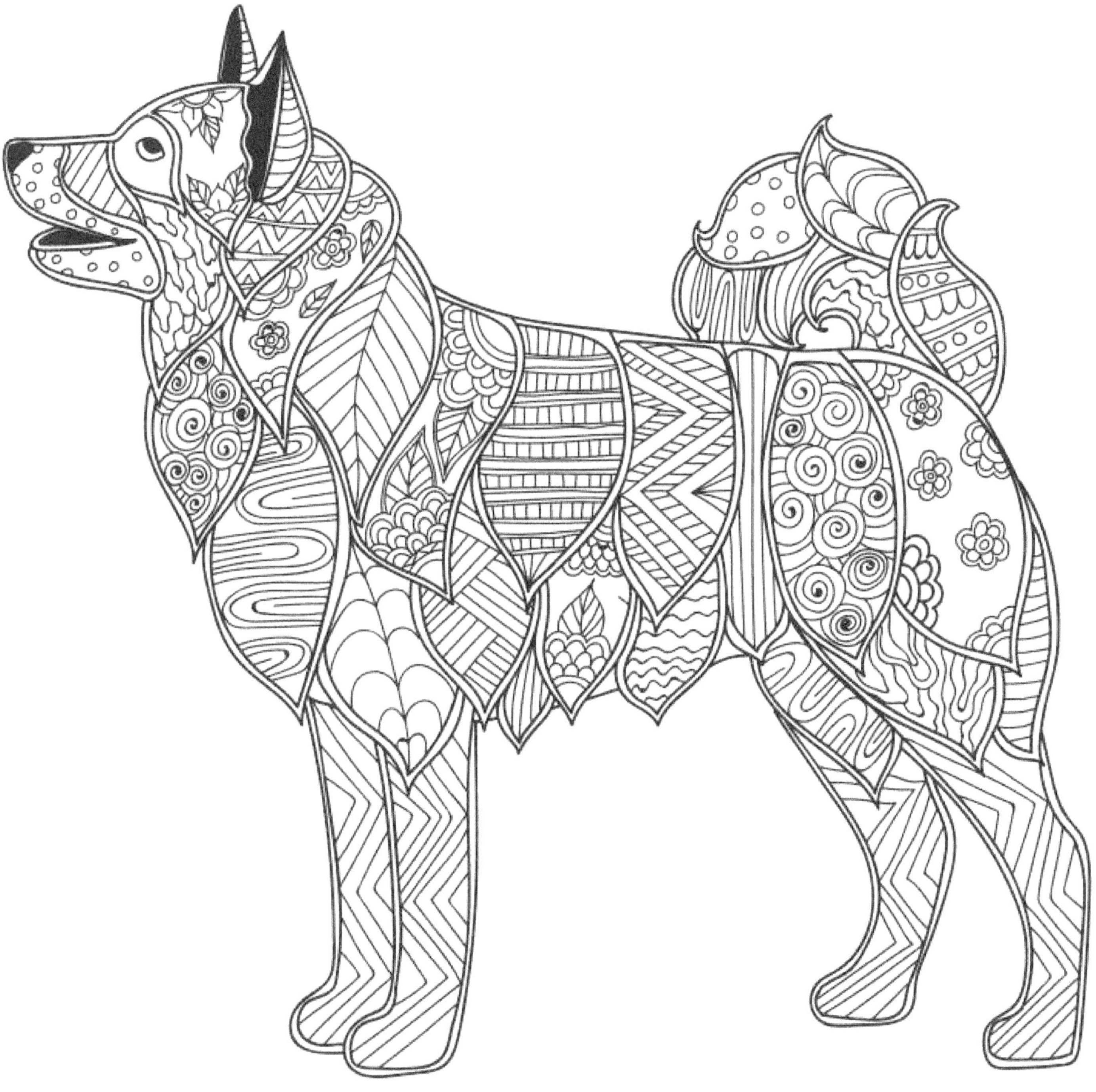

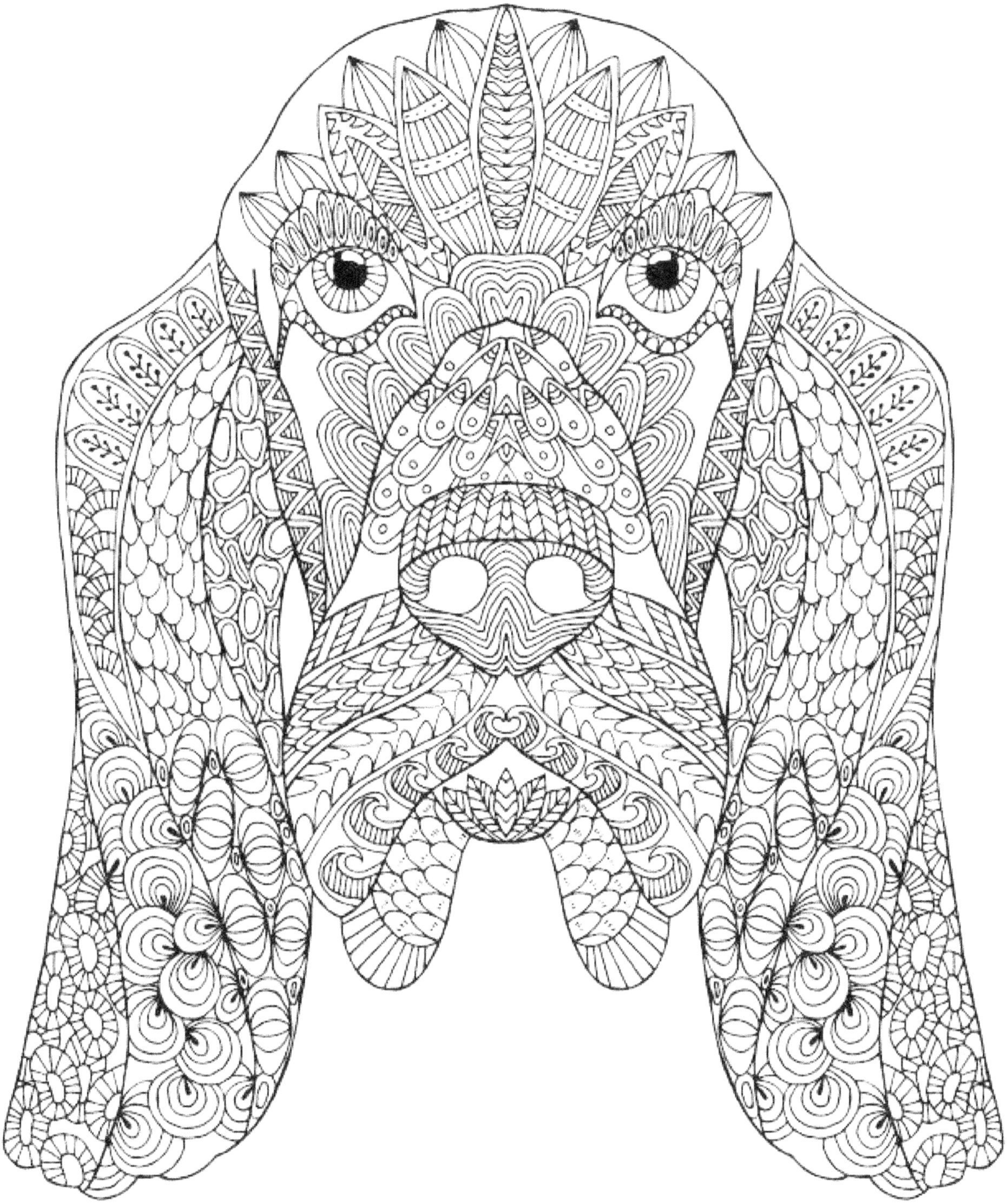

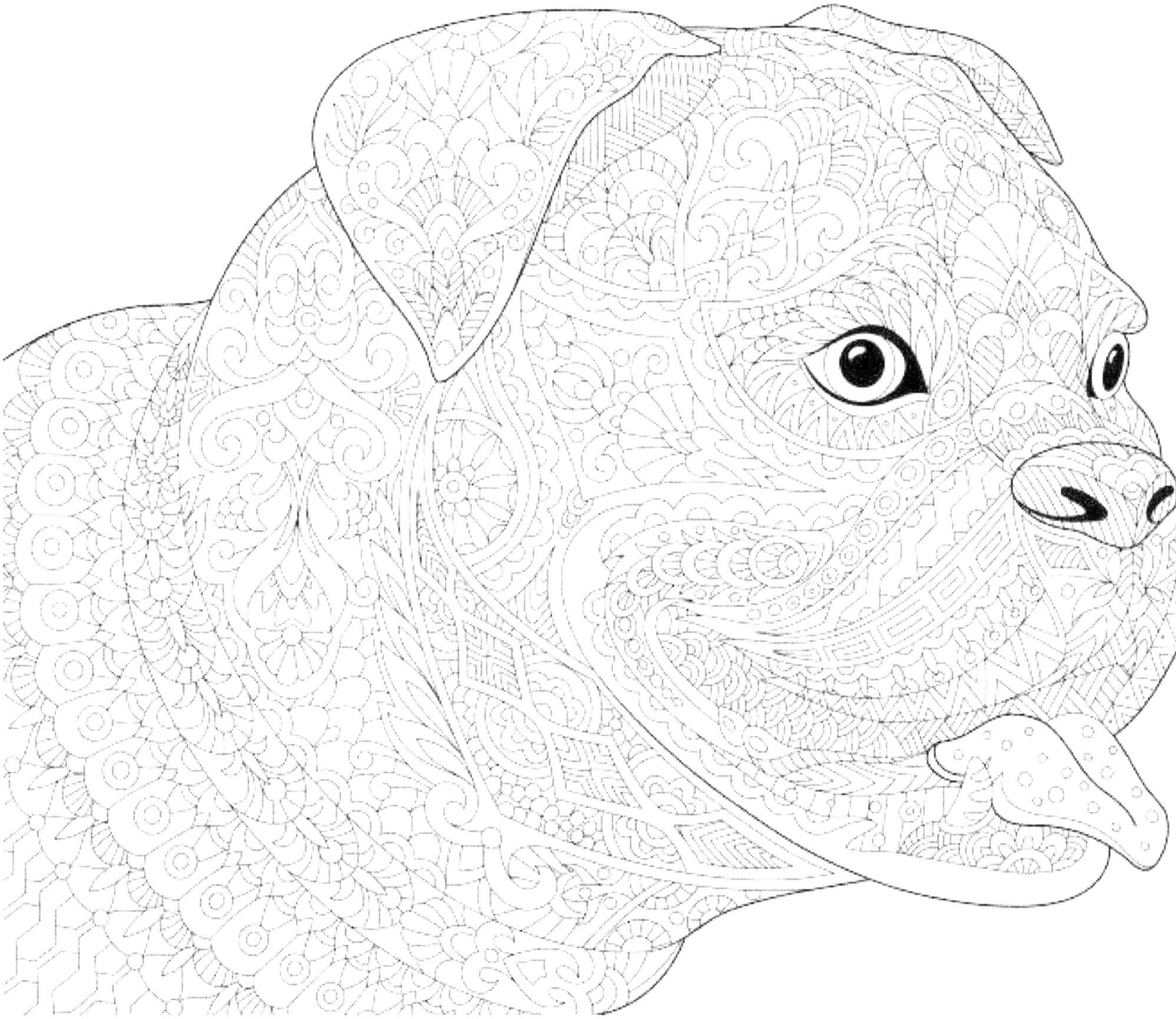

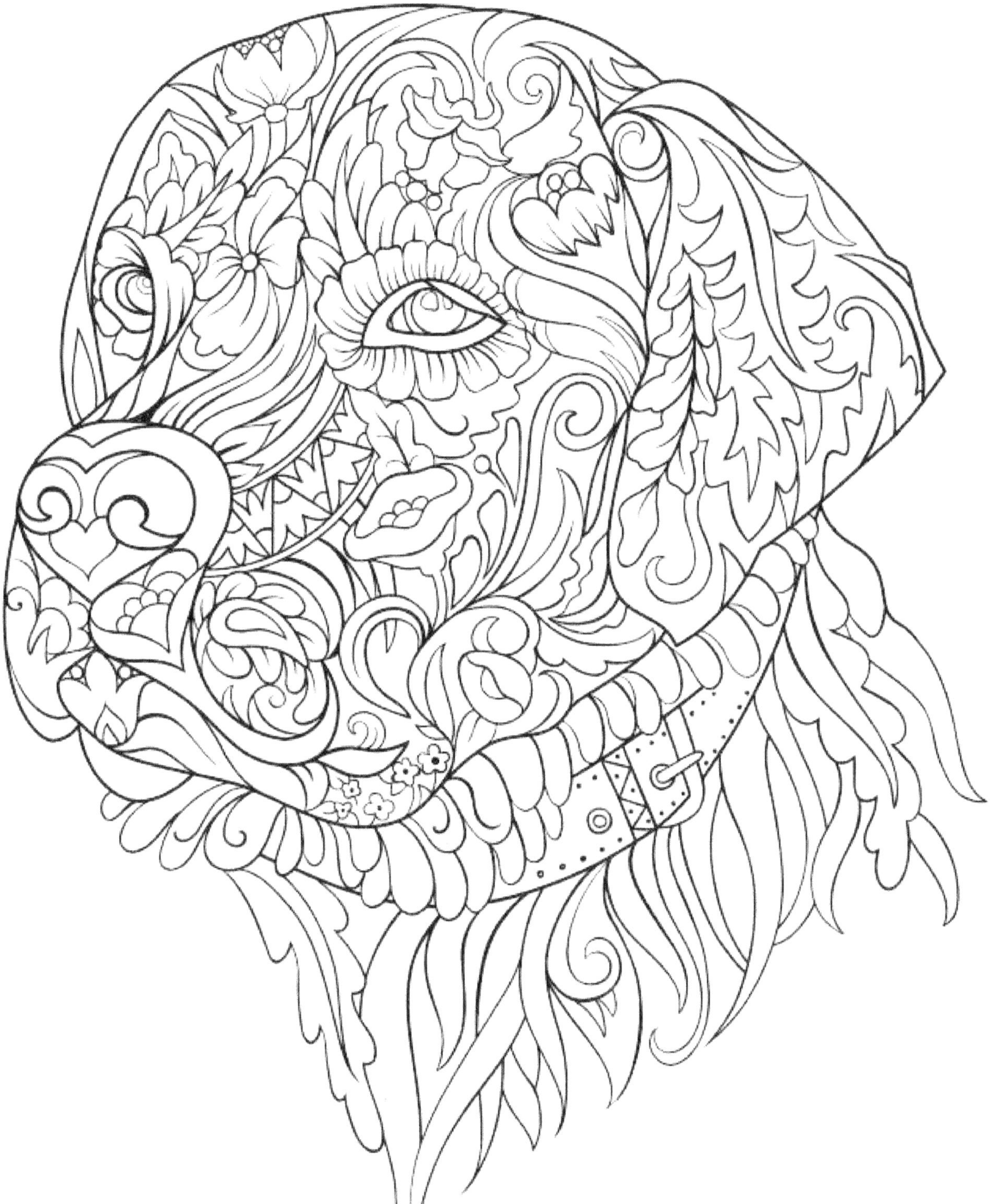

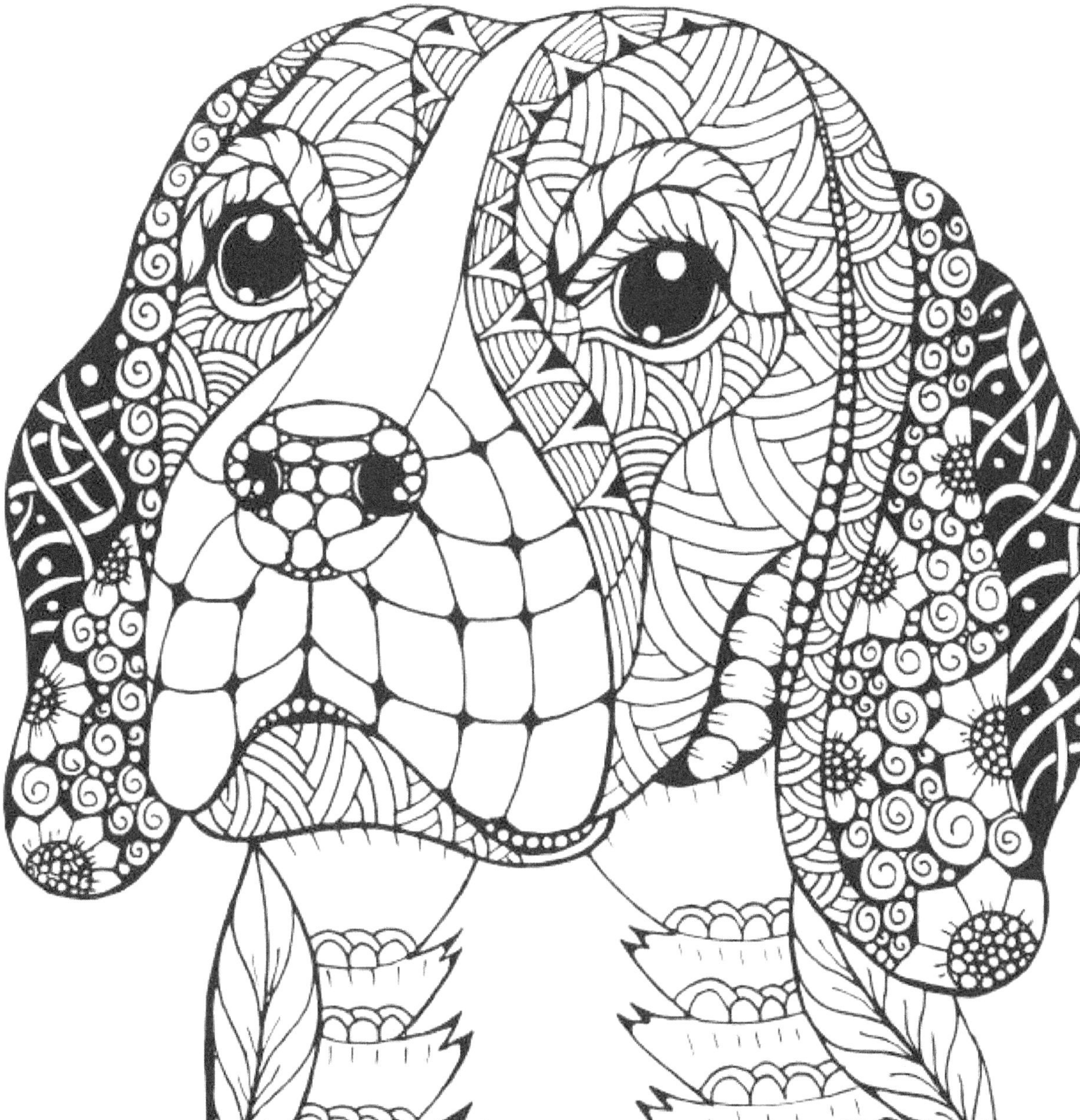

Surprise Bonus Sea Turtles Coloring Pages!

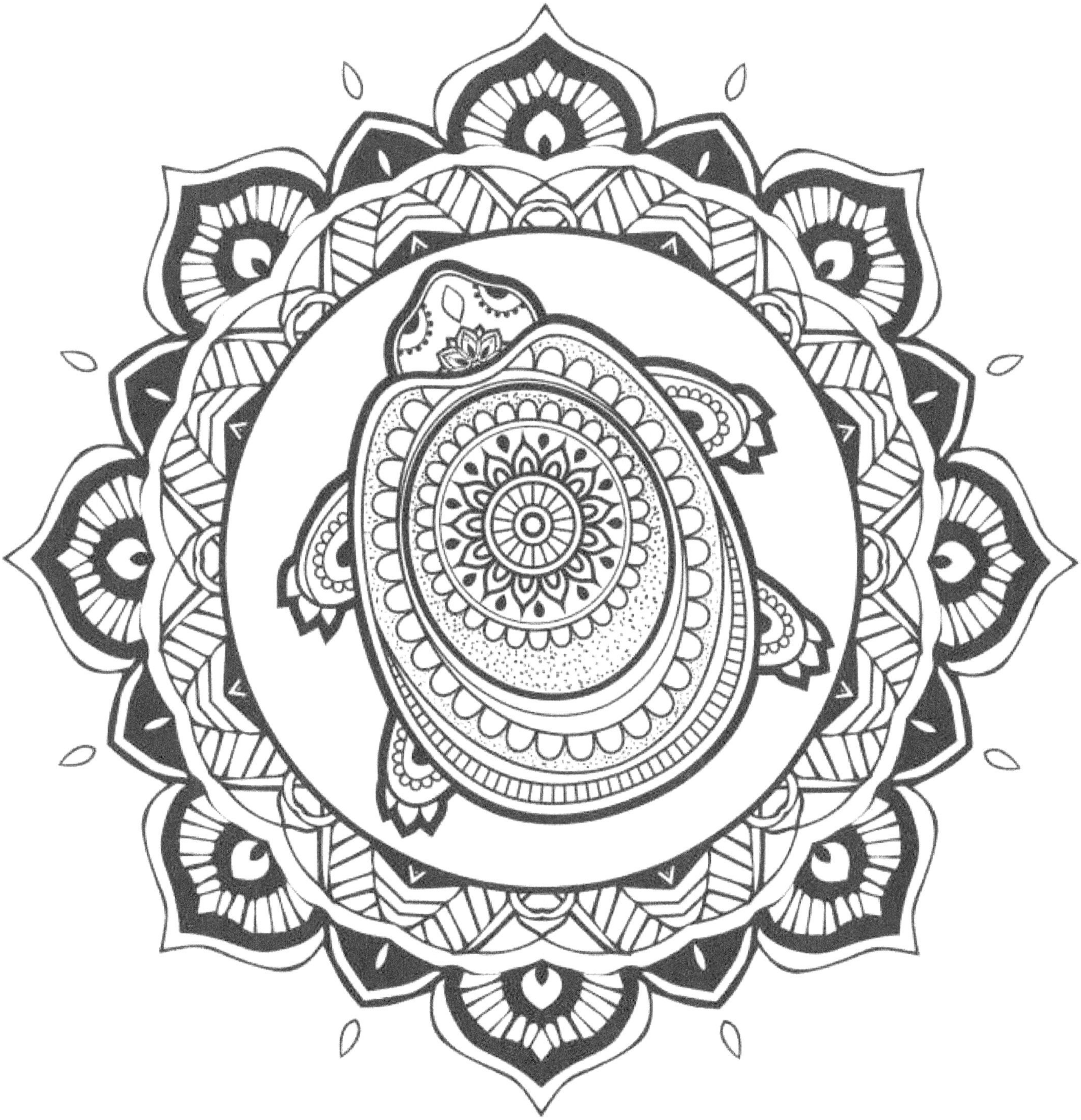

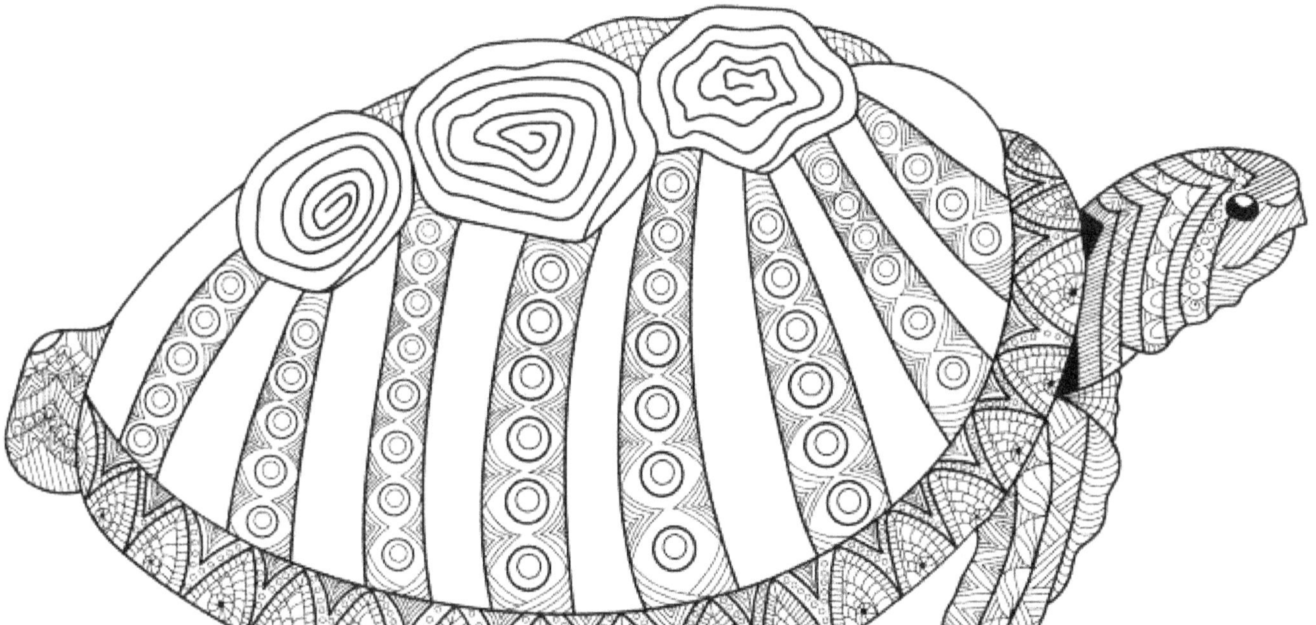

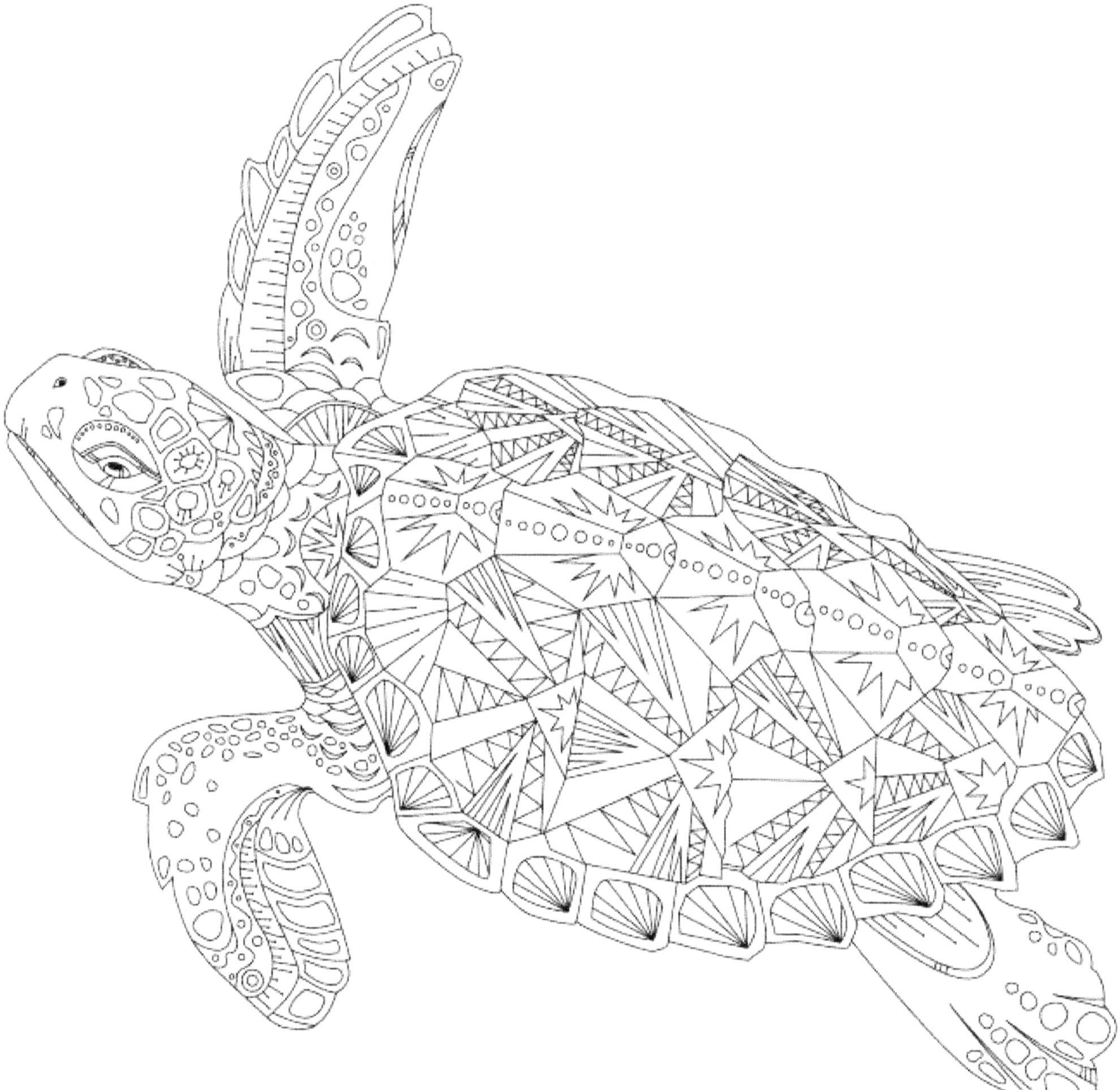

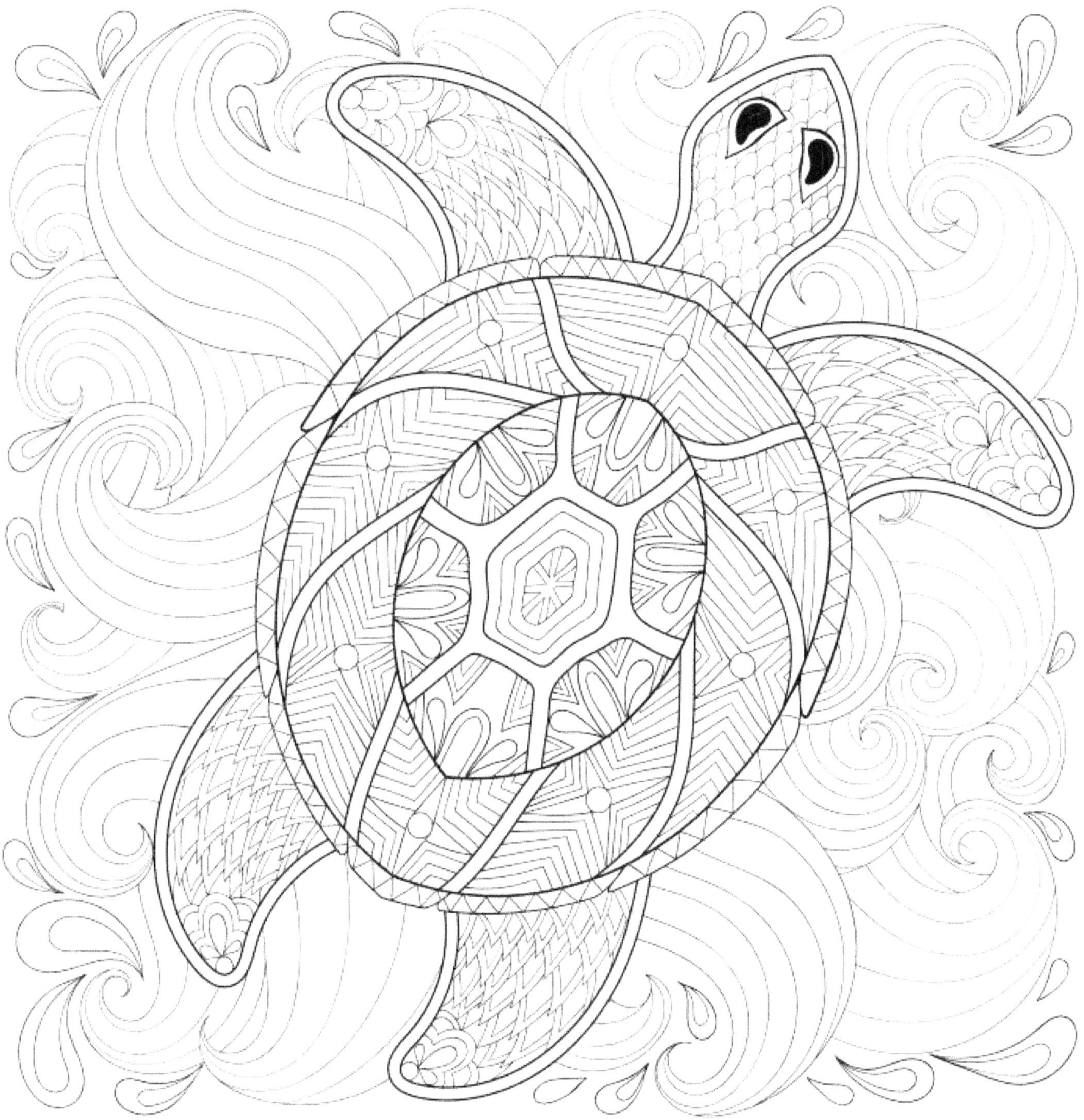

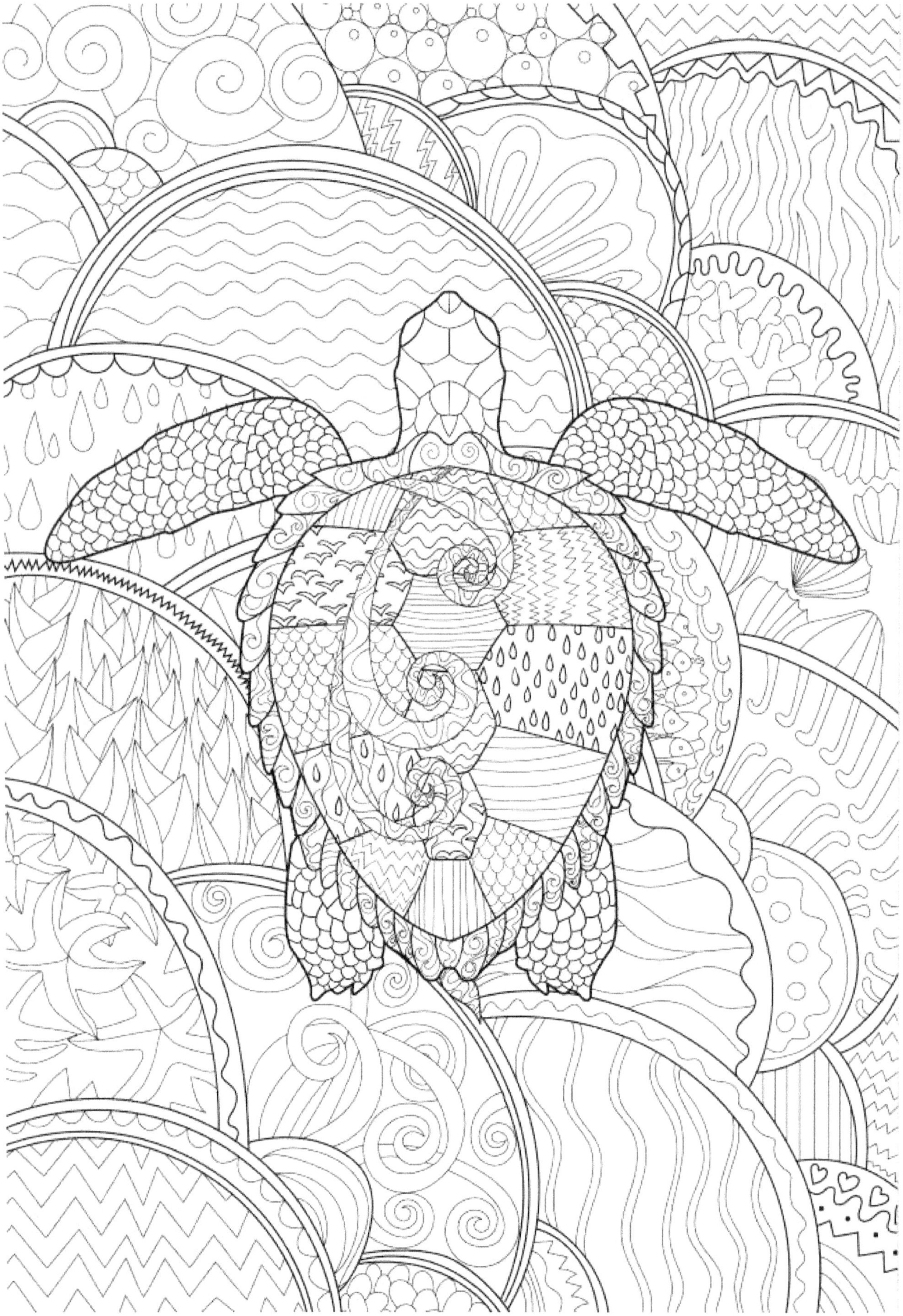

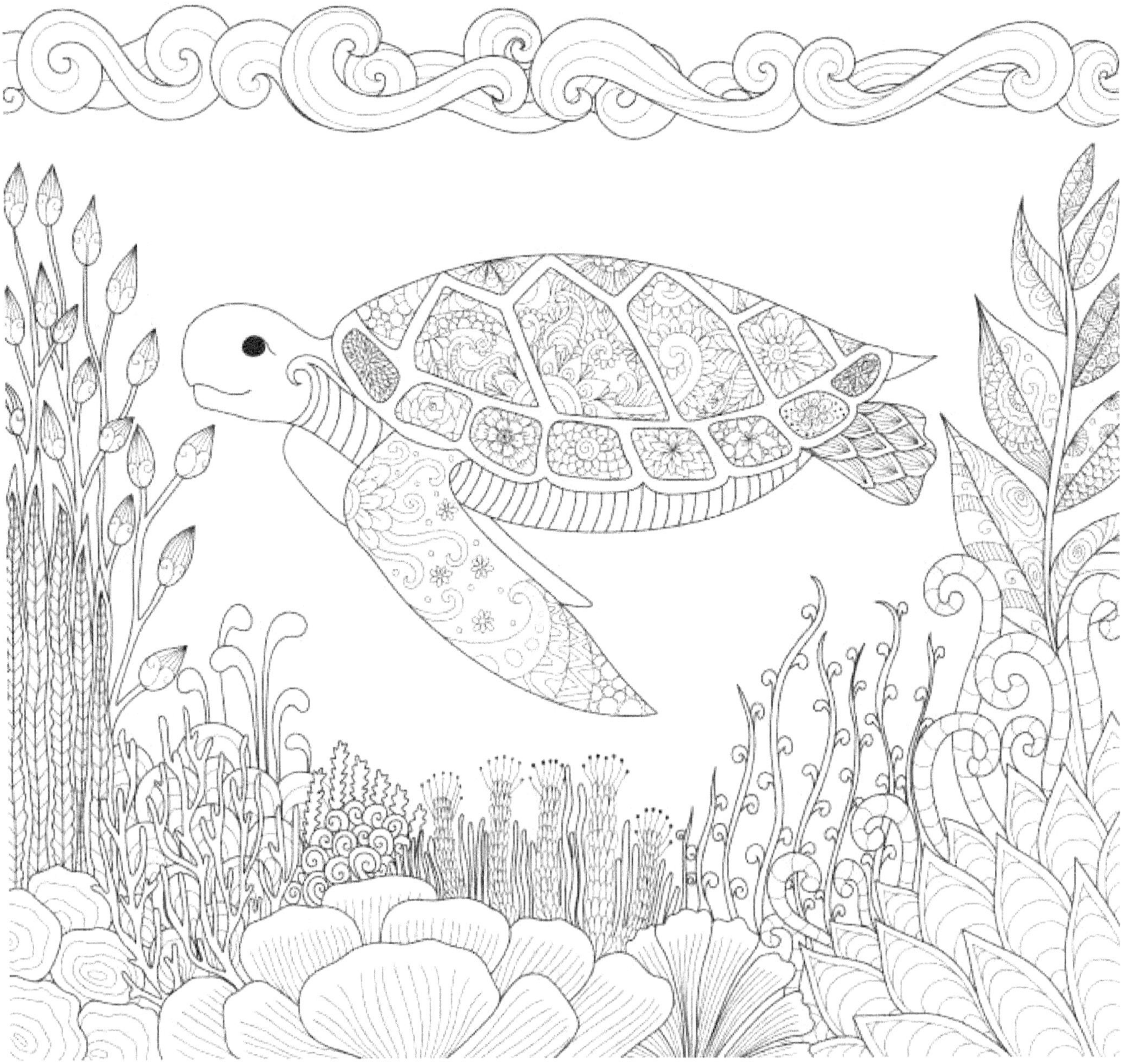

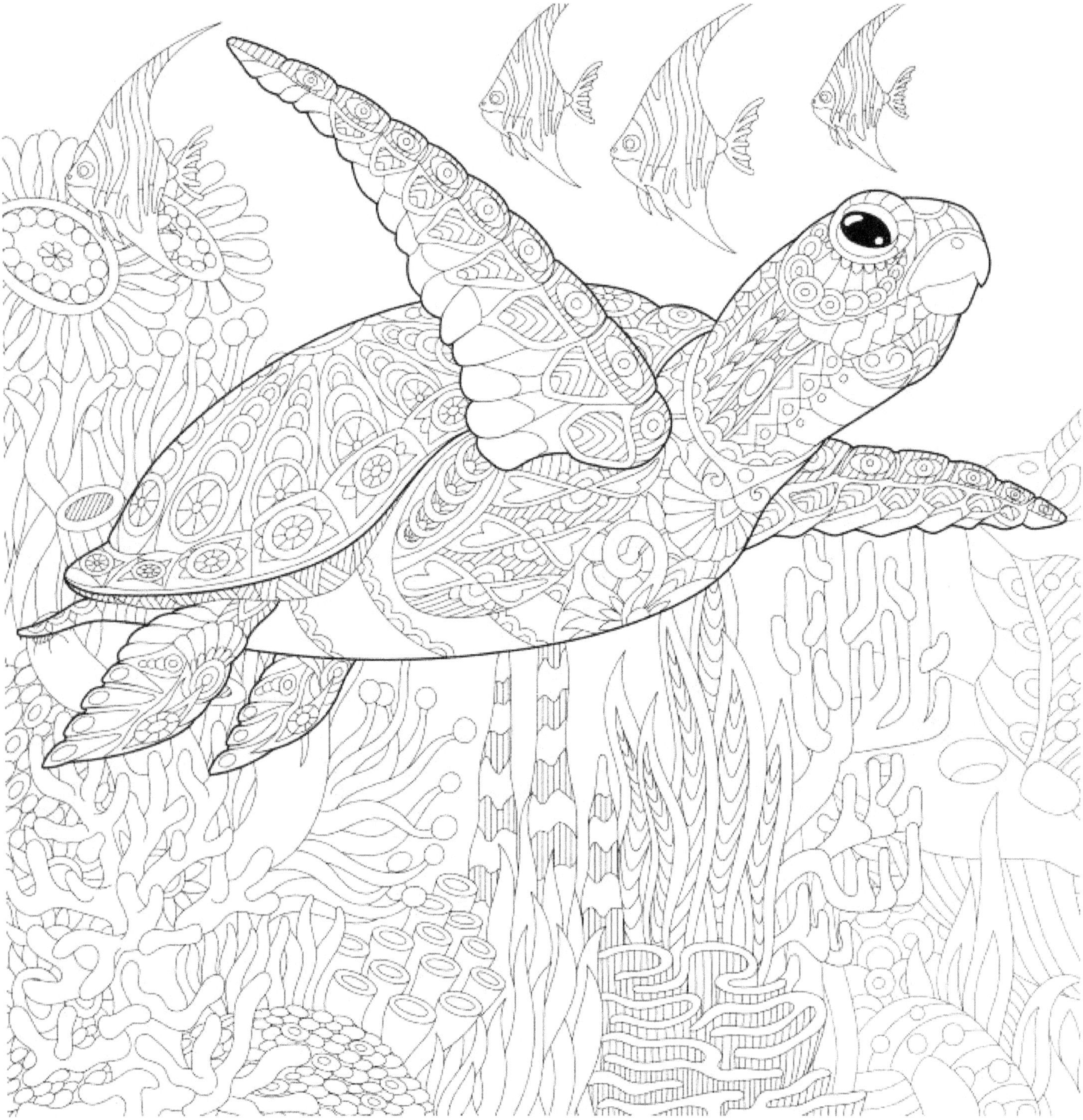

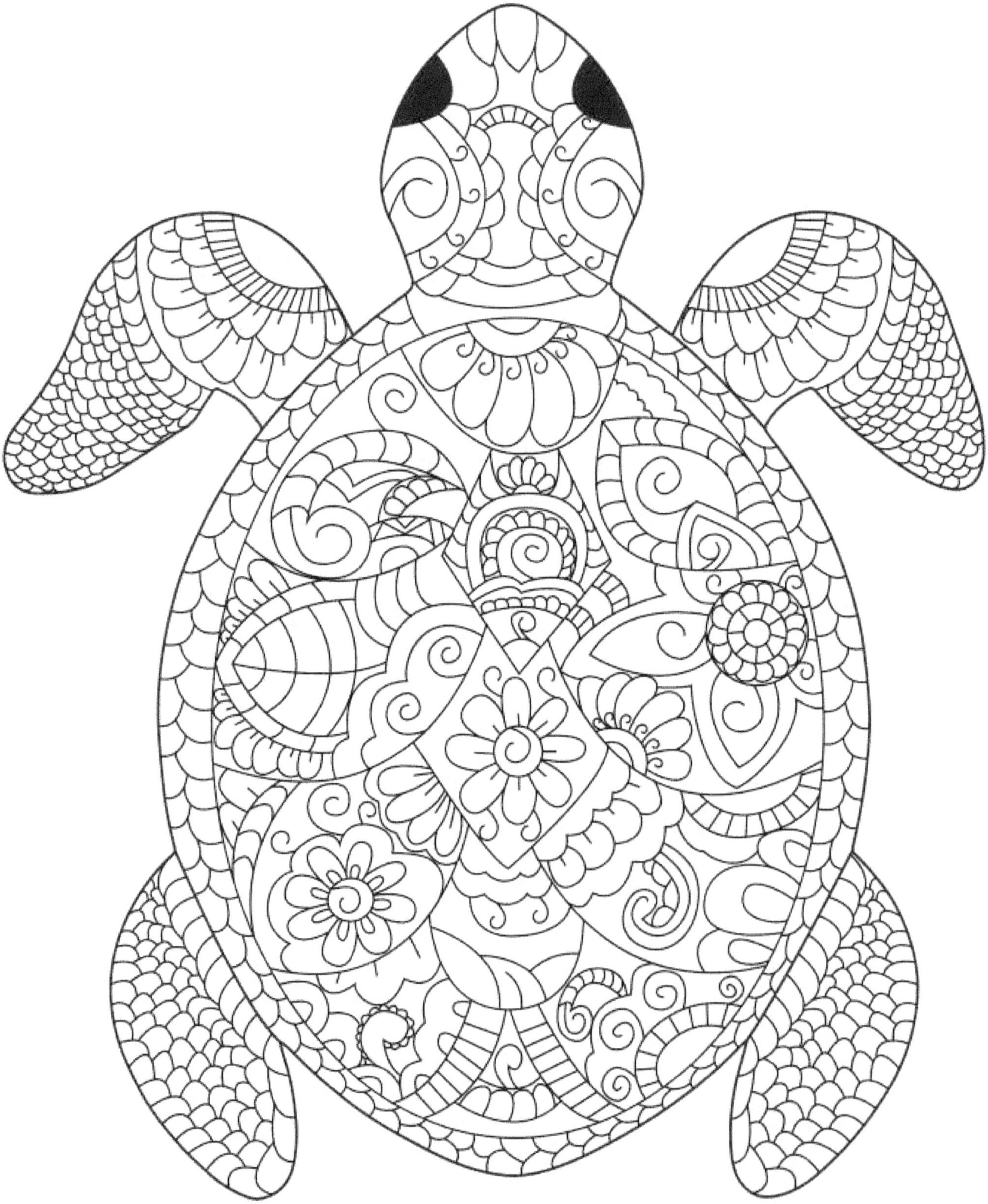

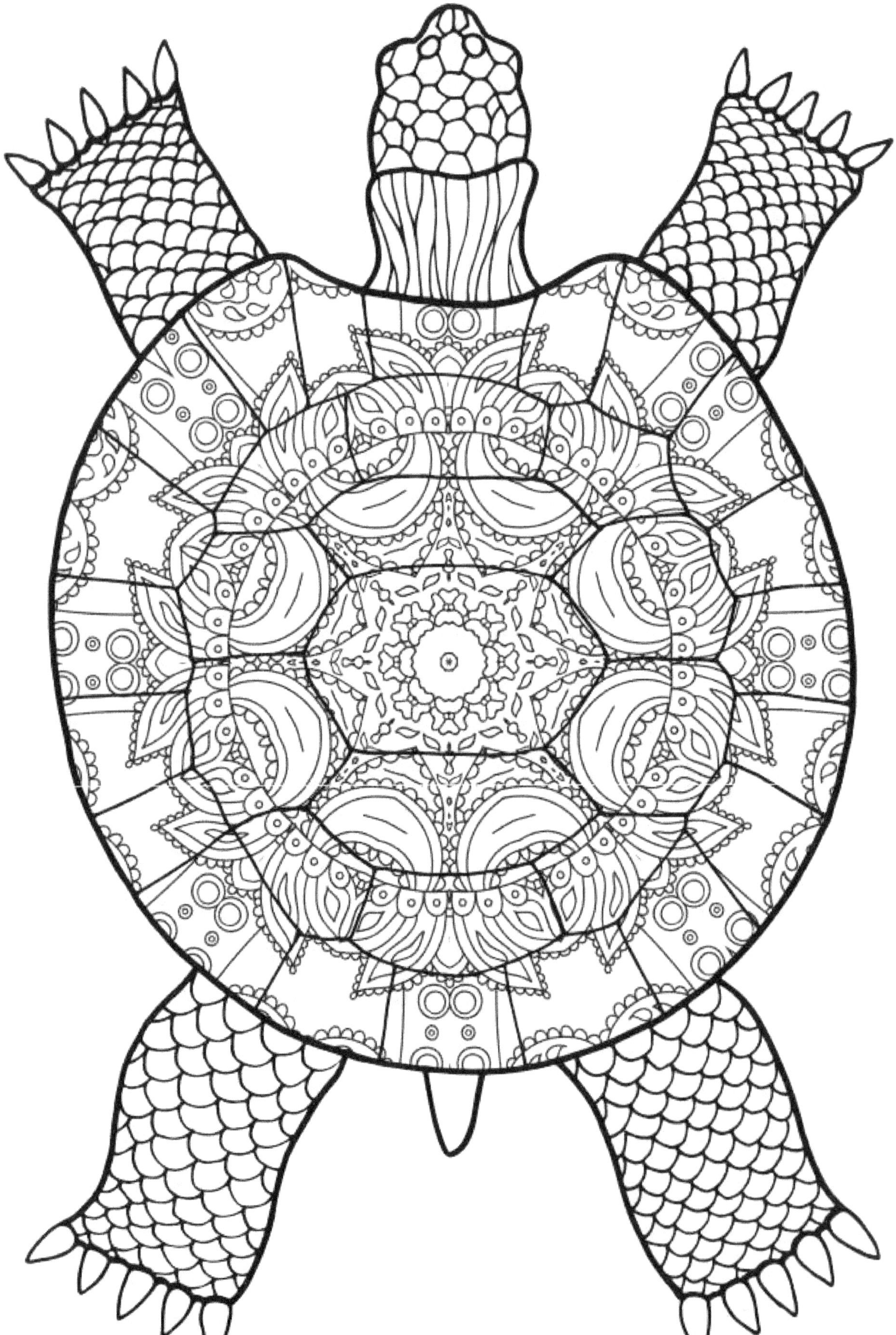

www.ingramcontent.com/pod-product-compliance
Lightning Source LLC
Chambersburg PA
CBHW081303180526
45170CB00007B/2545
9781546833536